SCHIRMER'S LIBRARY
OF MUSICAL CLASSICS

FELIX MENDELSSOHN-BARTHOLDY

Concertos

For the Piano

With the Orchestral Accompaniments
Arranged for a Second Piano by
ADOLF RUTHARDT

Op. 25, in G minor — Library Vol. 61

⟶ Op. 40, in D minor — Library Vol. 62

G. SCHIRMER, *Inc.*

DISTRIBUTED BY

 HAL•LEONARD®
CORPORATION

7777 W. BLUEMOUND RD. P.O. BOX 13819 MILWAUKEE, WI 53213

Concerto II.

The orchestra arranged for a Second Pianoforte.

F. MENDELSSOHN. Op. 40.

Composed 1837.
Published May, 1838.

The "Tutti" may be played by both pianos.

4

15731

16

15781

15731

15731

Finale.

Presto scherzando.

32

15731

15731

15731